Nikola Tesla Biography Book
by David Right

DEDICATION

PREFACE

Tesla was born in 1856 in Austria-Hungary and emigrated to the U.S. in 1884 as a physicist. In the late 1800's, Tesla was as well known as Thomas Edison. In some circles he was even more famous than Edison. Tesla is responsible for lot of the electrical equipment we have today. He invented the motor that is still used today. His inventions focused on magnetic forces and currents. He was very well thought of during the late 1800s.

Nikola Tesla in 1896, set up the system for the Niagara Falls hydroelectric plant. The first of its kind. The down fall of Nikola came when many of his patents were sold. In 1988 George Westinghouse, head of the Westinghouse Electric Company, purchased the patents to many of his electrical motor plans.

Nikola Tesla, also becomes known with many of our newer inventions. It is believed that Tesla set the foundation work for the further study and invention of the fluorescent light bulbs. It is also believed that he paved the way for the invention of RADAR tracking. Some of his technology is still in use today.

Who is Nikola Tesla is a question that is puzzling. He invented numerous projects in the late 1800s yet he died a poor man in a hotel room in 1943. After his death, the world honored him by naming the unit of magnetic flux density the "tesla."

Because he was so involved in this technology he was thought of as Thomas Edison's rival. Unfortunately Edison receives much more recognition than does Nikola Tesla in our history books!

Contents

CHAPTER 1- BIOGRAPHY OF NIKOLA TESLA

Nikola Tesla was born on July 10, 1856, in Smiljan, Lika, which was then part of the Austo-Hungarian Empire, region of Croatia. His father, Milutin Tesla was a Serbian Orthodox Priest and his mother Djuka Mandic was an inventor in her own right of household appliances. Tesla studied at the Realschule, Karlstadt in 1873, the Polytechnic Institute in Graz, Austria and the University of Prague. At first, he intended to specialize in physics and mathematics, but soon he became fascinated with electricity. He began his career as a electrical engineer with a telephone company in Budapest in 1881. It was there, as Tesla was walking with a friend through the city park that the elusive solution to the rotating magnetic field flashed through his mind. With a stick, he drew a diagram in the sand explaining to his friend the principle of the induction motor. Before going to America, Tesla joined Continental Edison Company in Paris where he designed dynamos. While in Strassbourg in 1883, he privately built a prototype of the induction motor and ran it successfully. Unable to interest anyone in Europe in promoting this radical device, Tesla accepted an offer to work for Thomas Edison in New York. His childhood dream was to come to America to harness the power of Niagara Falls.

Young Nikola Tesla came to the United States in 1884 with an introduction letter from Charles Batchelor to Thomas Edison: "I know two great men," wrote Batchelor, "one is you and the other is this young man." Tesla spent the next 59 years of his productive life living in New York. Tesla set about improving Edison's line of dynamos while working in Edison's lab in New Jersey. It was here that his divergence of opinion with Edison over direct current versus alternating current began. This disagreement climaxed in the war of the currents as Edison fought a losing battle to protect his investment in direct current equipment and facilities.

Nikola Tesla developed polyphase alternating current system of generators, motors and transformers and held 40 basic U.S. patents on the system, which George Westinghouse bought, determined to supply America with the Tesla system. Edison did not want to lose his DC empire, and a bitter war ensued. This was the war of the currents between AC and DC. Tesla -Westinghouse ultimatel emerged the victor because AC was a superior technology. It was a war won for the progress of both America and the world.

Tesla introduced his motors and electrical systems in a classic paper, "A New System of Alternating Current Motors and Transformers" which he delivered before the American Institute of Electrical Engineers in 1888. One of the most impressed was the industrialist and inventor George Westinghouse. One day he visited Tesla's laboratory and was amazed at what he saw. Tesla had constructed a model polyphase system consisting of an alternating current dynamo, step-up and step-down transformers and A.C. motor at the other end. The perfect partnership between Tesla and Westinghouse for the nationwide use of electricity in America had begun.

In February 1882, Tesla discovered the rotating magnetic field, a fundamental principle in physics and the basis of nearly all devices that use alternating current. Tesla brilliantly adapted the principle of rotating magnetic field for the construction of alternating current induction motor and the polyphase system for the generation, transmission, distribution and use of electrical power.

Tesla's A.C. induction motor is widely used throughout the world in industry and household appliances. It started the industrial revolution at the turn of the century. Electricity today is generated transmitted and converted to mechanical power by means of his inventions. Tesla's greatest achievement is his polyphase alternating current system, which is today lighting the entire globe.

Tesla astonished the world by demonstrating. the wonders of alternating current electricity at the World Columbian Exposition in Chicago in 1893. Alternating current became standard power in the 20th Century. This accomplishment changed the world. He designed the first hydroelectric powerplant in Niagara Falls in 1895, which was the final victory of alternating current. The achievement was covered widely in the world press, and Tesla was praised as a hero world wide. King Nikola of Montenegro conferred upon him the Order of Danilo.

In Colorado Springs, where he stayed from May 1899 until 1900, Tesla made what he regarded as his most important discovery-- terrestrial stationary waves.

By this discovery he proved that the Earth could be used as a conductor and would be as responsive as a tuning fork to electrical vibrations of a certain freuency. He also lighted 200 lamps without wires from a distance of 25 miles(40 kilometers) and created man-made lightning. At one time he was certain he had received signals from another planet in his Colorado laboratory, a claim that was met with disbelief in some scientific journals.

Financially supported by J. Pierpont Morgan, Tesla built the Wardenclyffe laboratory and its famous transmitting tower in Shoreham, Long Island between 1901 and 1905. This huge landmark was 187 feet high, capped by a 68-foot copper dome which housed the magnifying transmitter. It was planned to be the first broadcast system, transmitting both signals and power without wires to any point on the globe. The huge magnifying transmitter, discharging high freuency electricity, would turn the earth into a gigantic dynamo which would project its electricity in unlimited amounts anywhere in the world.

Because of a dispute between Morgan and Tesla as to the final use of the tower. Morgan withdrew his funds. The financier's classic comment was, "If anyone can draw on the power, where do we put the meter?

Tesla lectured to the scientific community on his inventions in New York, Philadelphia and St. Louis and before scientific organizations in both England and France in 1892. Tesla's lectures and writings of the 1890s aroused wide admiration among contemporaries popularized his inventions and inspired untold numbers of younger men to enter the new field of the radio and electrical science."

In 1894, he was given honorary doctoral degrees by Columbia and Yale University and the Elliot Cresson medal by the Franklin Institute. In 1934, the city of Philadelphia awarded him the John Scott medal for his polyphase power system. He was an honorary member of the National Electric Light Association and a fellow of the American Association for the Advancement of Science. On one occasion, he turned down an invitation from Kaiser Wilhelm II to come to Germany to demonstrate his experiments and to receive a high decoration.

In 1915, a New York Times article announced that Tesla and Edison were to share the Nobel Prize for physics. Oddly, neither man received the prize, the reason being unclear. It was rumored that Tesla refused the prize because he would not share with Edison, and because Marconi had already received his.

On his 75th birthday in 1931, the inventor appeared on the cover of Time Magazine. On this occasion, Tesla received congratulatory letters from more than 70 pioneers in science and engineering including Albert Einstein. These letters were mounted and presented to Tesla in the form of a testimonial volume.

 Tesla died on January 7th, 1943 in the Hotel New Yorker, where he had lived for the last ten years of his life. Room 3327 on the 33rd floor is the two-room suites he occupied.

A state funeral was held at St. John the Divine Cathedral in New York City. Telegrams of condolence were received from many notables, including the first lady Eleanor Roosevelt and Vice President Wallace. Over 2000 people attended, including several Nobel Laureates. He was cremated in Ardsley on the Hudson, New York. His ashes were interned in a golden sphere, Tesla's favorite shape, on permanent display at the Tesla Museum in Belgrade along with his death mask.

In his speech presenting Tesla with the Edison medal, Vice President Behrend of the Institute of Electrical Engineers eloquently expressed the following: "Were we to seize and eliminate from our industrial world the result of Mr. Tesla's work, the wheels of industry would cease to turn, our electric cars and trains would stop, our towns would be dark and our mills would be idle and dead. His name marks an epoch in the advance of electrical science." Mr. Behrend ended his speech with a paraphrase of Pope's lines on Newton: "Nature and nature's laws lay hid by night. God said 'Let Tesla be' and all was light."

"The world will wait a long time for Nikola Tesla's equal in achievement and imagination." E. ARMSTRONG

Nikola Tesla's Awards and Recognition

In 1917, Tesla was awarded the Edison Medal, the most coveted electrical prize in the United States.

Nikola Tesla's name has been honored with an International Unit of Magnetic Flux Density called "Tesla."

The United States Postal Service honored Tesla with a commemorative stamp in 1983.

Tesla was inducted into the Inventor's Hall of Fame in 1975.

The Nikola Tesla Award is one of the most distinguished honors presented by the Institute of Electrical Engineers. The award has been given annually since 1976.

The Nikola Tesla Statue is located on Goat Island to honor the man whose inventions were incorporated into the Niagara Falls Power Station in 1895. Tesla is known as the inventor of polyphase alternating current.

The Nikola Tesla Corner Sign, located at the intersection of 40th Street and 6th Avenue in Manhattan, is a constant reminder to all New Yorkers of the greatness of this genius.

CHAPTER 2- NIKOLA TESLA AND THOMAS EDISON RELATIONSHIP

The lives of Nikola Tesla and Thomas Edison, and the people they interacted with during their lifetimes, is an interesting story. Nikola Tesla and Thomas Edison were two of the most prolific inventors of the twentieth century.

Tesla came to America looking for Edison and hoping to earn his respect, and show him his inventions in the field of AC (alternating current). The arrogant Edison brushed away Tesla as an intelligent man with ideas that weren't practical, because Edison favored the competing system DC (direct current).

Tesla, jilted by Edison, would go out on his own to prove his point. Years later Tesla would team up with Edison's rival, George Westinghouse, and together they would defeat Edison in a great science and technology feud known as The War of Currents.

In the battle of the two crazy mad scientists, Tesla would be the ultimate victor in the battle of good versus evil, defeating his rival, Edison. Much of what is said is exaggerated for the sake of a good story. The myths and legends grow stronger every day on the internet.

The goal of History is to be fanatic at finding the truth. There are so many myths and legends about Tesla, we could write an entire book of debunking all the misinformation. For the sake of setting the record straight in the battle of Edison versus Tesla, we needed to at least address some of the major points of misinformation and put some things into perspective.

The often quoted myth states that Tesla died in 1934 a broke and broken old man because Edison stole Tesla's ideas. The statement becomes the mantra to make Tesla the patron saint of geeks and a martyr. The statement perpetuates many myths about the life of Tesla being one of hardships and failures.

Exactly what ideas of Tesla did Edison steal?

During the time Tesla worked for Edison they were on different sides of the argument. Tesla hoped to show Edison his ideas on AC (alternating current) but Edison refused to look at them because he was pushing for DC (direct current) as the preferred method of electrical power distribution. Tesla's patents on AC (alternating current) were purchased by George Westinghouse, and Tesla worked with Westinghouse to defeat Edison in the War of Currents.

The myth that Edison stole Tesla's ideas is rooted in Edison's legacy of creating an invention factory where Edison used his staff to develop ideas and turn them into patents. Some point to the concept of the invention factory as the reason for his success, critics say Edison took his invention factory too far, and Edison took credit for any individual creativity by his employees. How is Edison's invention factory any different than the large number of engineers, designers, and programmers working for Microsoft or Apple, but all we hear about is the success of Bill Gates or Steve Jobs? How many inventions and innovations made in the name of Apple or Microsoft were not the direct work of Gates or Jobs?

Tesla died broke because of Edison?

The myth making Tesla a martyr, that he died a broke and broken old man because of Edison, is a total head scratcher. In the war of currents, the battle of AC versus DC, Tesla was victorious. In the 1890s. Tesla defeated Edison teamed up with George Westinghouse and was paid well for his efforts. I've seen remarks made on the internet such as "Tesla was cheated by both Edison and Westinghouse and died in poverty."

Tesla was a humble and broken old man?

Critics of Edison have said that Edison's greatest invention was his own fame. Fans of Tesla paint a picture of a humble and broken old man that didn't seek fame. Tesla was at just as much a showman and pitchman as Edison and he understood how to work a crowd. Tesla hung out at New Yorks finest restaurants mixing it up the New York elite. That's how he would meet his famous investors like J.P Morgan and John Jacob Astor.

In 1899, Tesla used money he received from John Jacob Astor IV, one of the richest people in the world at the time, to build a new laboratory in Colorado Springs. Various accounts say that Astor was not happy with Tesla, and thought he was deceived. Astor thought he was investing in a new lighting system, but Tesla used the money to fund his Colorado Springs experiments. In 1900, Tesla convinced John Pierpont "J.P." Morgan to invest $150,000 in him so he could build a trans-Atlantic wireless communication system. J.P. Morgan had significant influence in the world of corporate finance the early 1900s. Tesla lost favor with J.P. Morgan for similar reasons to his falling out with John Jacob Astor IV. Morgan believed that Tesla did not use the money for the purpose of his original request.

In 1918, Tesla moves to the Hotel St. Regis. After running up a balance of over $3,000, he was forced to leave. Tesla moved to the luxurious Hotel Marguery on the west side of Park Avenue. In 1925, Tesla rented another room at the Hotel Pennsylvania while continuing to rent the room at Hotel Marguery. Tesla had many pigeons he fed and cared for, in 1930 Tesla was asked to leave the Hotel Pennsylvania after residents complained about the droppings from his pets, and he fell behind in his rent. In 1930, moved to the Hotel Governor Clinton. Once again falling behind in his rent Tesla was forced to move.

Various accounts claim different reasons for the Westinghouse Corporation coming to Tesla's rescue, but Tesla would move to the Hotel New Yorker in 1934, with the rent paid for by Westinghouse. One story is that Tesla was hit by a taxi on the streets of New York and injured, Westinghouse executives agreed to pay his room and board for the remainder of his life.

For much of his life spent living in New York, Tesla moved from one upscale hotel to another. If you look at what Tesla received for his work with Westinghouse, along with the investment money from Astor and Morgan, he received the modern day equivalent of several million dollars. While the story of his life may tell us he died broke, it does not paint the picture of someone who lived in poverty and never got a fair break.

Why is Thomas Edison more famous than Nikola Tesla?

There are various reasons why Thomas Edison became more famous than Nikola Tesla. Edison developed close lifelong friendships with some of the most powerful and influential people around in his day such as Henry Ford. Without going off on a Henry Ford tangent, it's safe to say that Ford, like Edison, was a media superstar in his day. At times Tesla had the respect of the most powerful and influential people around in his day, such as J.P. Morgan and John Jacob Astor IV, but would lose favor with them over time.

Even if Edison wasn't as smart as Tesla he wasn't a fool. In the case of many inventions, it goes beyond just having an idea. Sometimes it even goes beyond building a prototype and proving the concept. Edison did not invent the electric light bulb, but he was able to develop a light bulb that was practical. Lot of the legacy of both Thomas Edison and Henry Ford has to do with the image they created for themselves. Edison and Ford build companies, they forged partnerships. Some people see capitalism as inherently evil. If that is true, it is a necessary evil.

In the PBS documentary "Tesla Master of Lightning" Tesla's grand-nephew William Terbo explains the downfall of Nikola Tesla. "He was totally disinterested in business. He did not make the relationship between the importance of business and the importance of his invention and discovery."

Many of the things that Tesla allegedly invented were not developed in a university laboratory where the processes were witnessed by experts or scholars, they were not in the course of business, as was the case with Edison and Ford. Tesla preferred to work out theories with experiments before implementing it with physical designs. Tesla created small private laboratories with a small staff where he was in total control.

A New York Times □uote from Tesla on the death of Edison underscore the differences between the two inventors: "If he had a needle to find in a haystack he would not stop to reason where it was most likely to be, but would proceed at once, with the feverish diligence of a bee, to examine straw after straw until he found the object of his search. I was almost a sorry witness of such doings, knowing that a little theory and calculation would have saved him ninety per cent of his labor. "

Tesla was one of a small group of engineers working on AC in America in the mid 1880s, but he was not the only one. Many of the "inventions" of Nikola Tesla were not the sole idea of Tesla but were one of many scientists and inventors. When Tesla teamed up with Westinghouse, the concept of AC power generation was already being developed by the Westinghouse company, Tesla helped to improve upon the process and the product. His partnership with Westinghouse was his greatest success. It was also one of the few times where Tesla was on a team, rather than working alone.

In our next chapter, I will take a look at Tesla's relationship with inventor and entrepreneur George Westinghouse. When the phrase "War of Currents" is mentioned most people are quick to say that was the great battle between Edison and Tesla. What often gets lost in the conversation is that Tesla and George Westinghouse worked together to win over Edison.

The legacy and legend of Nikola Tesla

 There is so many claims to who invented what, we have not even touched on Tesla's claims to inventing radio, x-rays, and death rays. We could show a long list of inventions by Tesla, as well as Edison, and illustrate the discoveries that came before them. But that does not change the fact that Edison and Tesla were both visionaries. Both men had their own way of looking at things and coming up with ways to improve upon them.

We are not trying to take anything away from the accomplishments of Nikola Tesla. The constant bickering on who was the better inventor, followed by endless rants of misinformation, serves no purpose. Some of the conspiracy theories about why Tesla failed get pretty wild. There are those that point to the government who shut Tesla down because of his death ray that would end all wars.

CHAPTER 3- NIKOLA TESLA AND WESTINGHOUSE RELATIONSHIP

George Westinghouse, (born Oct. 6, 1846, Central Bridge, N.Y., U.S.—died March 12, 1914, New York City), American inventor and industrialist who was chiefly responsible for the adoption of alternating current for electric power transmission in the United States.

After serving in both the U.S. Army and the navy in the Civil War, Westinghouse received his first patent in late 1865 for a rotary steam engine. Though the engine proved impractical, he later applied the same principle to develop a water meter. In that same year he invented a device for placing derailed freight cars back on their tracks.

In November and December of 1887, Nikola Tesla, a Serbian engineer, filed for seven U.S. patents in the field of polyphase AC motors and power transmission. His motor produced alternating current and his transformers stepped up and stepped down the voltage as required. Westinghouse believed in Tesla's inventions, installed, them in the Adams Station and brought electricity to Buffalo.

He purchased the patents of Nikola Tesla's AC motor and hired Tesla to improve and modify the motor for use in his power system. When the system was ready for the American market, the advocates of DC power immediately set out to discredit AC power. Their attacks culminated in charges that the use of AC power was a menace to human life; to support their argument, they introduced a standard Westinghouse AC generator as the official means of executing death sentences in the state of New York. This tactic was insufficient to suppress AC power, however, and in 1893 the Westinghouse company was retained to light the World's Columbian Exposition at Chicago. In addition, Westinghouse secured the rights to develop the great falls of the Niagara River with AC generators.

The challenge

To send electricity over long distances requires high voltage to "push" the current through wires. Yet using high voltages in homes and factories can be dangerous.

With a transformer, alternating current (AC) can easily be "stepped up" to high voltages for transmission, or "stepped down" to lower voltages for manufacturing and domestic uses. This cannot be done with direct current (DC).

Westinghouse VS. Edison

George Westinghouse's firm faith in the AC system led to the founding of the Westinghouse Electric Company in 1886, to oppose the DC system supported by Edison. Westinghouse's company deliberately underbid and won the contract to power the 1893 World's Columbian Exposition in Chicago. The widely publicized implementation of AC converted skeptics, like Lord Kelvin, and forced them to recognize the system's potential.

Based on this success, the Cataract Company hired Westinghouse to build 5,000 horsepower generators for the Adams Station

CHAPTER 4- INVENTIONS OF NIKOLA TESLA THAT CHANGE THE WORLD

Nikola Tesla is a famous inventor, Tesla's inventions help make the world what it is today. His inventions are known by everyone, but often attributed so some else who's undeserving of the credit. He was an electrical engineer, mechanical engineer, physicist, and futurists. Some of the inventions that make our life so easy can be attributed to him and his ideas are still revolutionizing the world today.

Perhaps the most famous and widely used of Tesla's inventions, alternating current or AC, has revolutionized the modern world, and without our daily lives would be completely different. This invention led to a famous war between Tesla and Edison. Edison preferred DC over AC, even though DC was more dangerous. Edison was determined to prove to the world that his way was superior and put on a dishonest demonstration to try and illustrate that. During the demonstration he attempted to paint AC as the more dangerous option and electrocuted an elephant in public to try and prove his point. Tesla demonstrated many times that AC was harmless by sending electricity through his own body to produce light.

Tesla invented the radio in 1897. He sent a wireless transmission from his lab to a robotic boat that was 40 km away, to be able to this in 1897 is extraordinary. He invented the basic design for it all the way back to 1892, and finally patented his working invention in 1898. Using radio transmissions Tesla managed to direct a remote control boat from 40 km (25 miles) away. It was breakthrough technology and made front page news. Unfortunately like many of his Tesla's inventions the credit was stolen by man named Guglielmo Marconi who is commonly believed to have invented it years later. Edison actually would have finished inventing the product even sooner if not for a fire that desolated his lab in 1895.

The robotic boat which he invented was actually the world's first robot, and Tesla is even known as the father of Robotics because of it. Tesla saw a future for robotics which many people still don't believe could be a reality. He saw a future where humanoid robot would do all the manual labour jobs creating a safer world for people. This prophecy has partly come true, robots are a large part of many industries including space exploration and medicine. Without Tesla's inventions in robotics the world may be a very different place.

The wireless energy transfer;Tesla invented a way of transferring energy wirelessly, by firing up a series of phosphorus light bulbs using electrodynamic induction. The potential of this is the ability to transfer energy to different places all over the world, giving us the ability to power things from across the globe without even having to go near it. This could allow us to supply poor areas with the energy they need to survive, and live well. The technology has already started being looked into by phone companies who want to use it to power people's phones wherever they are. There have already been multiple products that successfully use this technology to power things wirelessly and without the use of Cables.

Tesla invented the electric motor but it didn't become popular until very recently thanks to Elon Musk. Tesla had the plan for his AC motor in his head until he had an opportunity to build the actual model. The alternating current created magnetic poles that reversed themselves without the use of mechanics. This caused the armature to spin around the motor. These motors are now used in many different household appliances like fans. The existence of rotating magnetic fields was first proposed by Francois Arago, a French Physicist, in 1824. Tesla and Galileo Ferraris demonstrated the first working AC motors independently in the 1880's.

Tesla started researching X-ray technology in 1894, which he described at the time as radiant energy of invisible kinds". He first discovered the energy when he noticed damage had been done to film in his lab, which may have been related to experiments he did involving a Crookes tube. It's possible that he actually managed to capture an X-ray image when taking a picture of mark Twain illuminated by a Geissler tube. This happened only few weeks before the discovery of X-ray was announced by Willhelm Rontgen. Lot of Tesla's research, which was worth an enourmous amount was lost in a laboratory fire in 1895.

While working on the radio Tesla also invented the first remote control. He used t to control a small remote control boat which he used in demonstration in

1898. This demonstration showed that he could use a remote control to wirelessly send radio transmissions to control a boat and dictate the direction in which it moves. Tesla named it teleautomaton. This is easily one of the most successful and widely used of Tesla's inventions, unfortunately like most of his inventions barely anyone knows he invented it. Many of the spectators watching Tesla's inventions, didn't believe that it was really happening at first, and some claimed that he was cheating, some even claimed that he had trained little monkeys to sail the boat from the inside.

One of his most famous inventions is the Tesla Coil which uses two coils, a primary and a secondary, and each using an independent capacitor, which stored energy. Between the coils is a open gap, which is waiting to be filled with electricity created by the device. Using this device you can create bolts of lightning, create electron winds, and send currents of electricity throughout your body. The Tesla coils main purpose in the modern world is simply to entertain, and satisfy curiosity about the invention, but it is also used in radios, and there is even a lighter on Amazon which can be bought that uses the technology.

The Adams Power Plant was a hydroelectric plant that harnessed the power of Niagara falls using Nikola Tesla's ideas. The Niagara Falls commission was looking for a company that would be able to build a hydroelectric plant capable of harnessing it's power, and at first considered Thomas Edison's DC plant, but decided to go with Westinghouse Electrics, which used AC. At first people were sceptical it would work and funding was scarce, but after people realized how effective it was funding wasn't hard to come by.

One of the most fascinating, mysterious, and controversial of Tesla's inventions was his earthquake machine. A small oscillating device which he claimed could bring down an entire building of any size given enough time. He used the machine in his lab and almost destroyed the entire building. The device was tiny but when timed at the perfect frequency could add a little more energy to the wave of flex to the building with each little vibration. Tesla was terrified of what the device could potentially be used for, and decided to take a hammer and destroy the device. He ordered his assistants to claim that they had no idea what could have caused the shaking and the tremors.

CHAPTER 5- THE RISE AND FALL OF NIKOLA TESLA AND HIS TOWER

By the end of his brilliant and tortured life, the Serbian physicist, engineer and inventor Nikola Tesla was penniless and living in a small New York City hotel room. He spent days in a park surrounded by the creatures that mattered most to him—pigeons—and his sleepless nights working over mathematical equations and scientific problems in his head. That habit would confound scientists and scholars for decades after he died, in 1943. His inventions were designed and perfected in his imagination.

Tesla believed his mind to be without equal, and he wasn't above chiding his contemporaries, such as Thomas Edison, who once hired him. "If Edison had a needle to find in a haystack," Tesla once wrote, "he would proceed at once with the diligence of the bee to examine straw after straw until he found the object of his search. I was a sorry witness of such doing that a little theory and calculation would have saved him ninety percent of his labor."

But what his contemporaries may have been lacking in scientific talent (by Tesla's estimation), men like Edison and George Westinghouse clearly possessed the one trait that Tesla did not—a mind for business.

And in the last days of America's Gilded Age, Nikola Tesla made a dramatic attempt to change the future of communications and power transmission around the world. He managed to convince J.P. Morgan that he was on the verge of a breakthrough, and the financier gave Tesla more than $150,000 to fund what would become a gigantic, futuristic and startling tower in the middle of Long Island, New York. In 1898, as Tesla's plans to create a worldwide wireless transmission system became known, Wardenclyffe Tower would be Tesla's last chance to claim the recognition and wealth that had always escaped him.

Nikola Tesla was born in modern-day Croatia in 1856; his father, Milutin, was a priest of the Serbian Orthodox Church. From early age, he demonstrated the obsessiveness that would puzzle and amuse those around him. He could memorize entire books and store logarithmic tables in his brain. He picked up languages easily, and he could work through days and nights on only few hours sleep.

At the age of 19, he was studying electrical engineering at the Polytechnic Institute at Graz in Austria, where he quickly established himself as a star student. He found himself in an ongoing debate with a professor over perceived design flaws in the direct-current (DC) motors that were being demonstrated in class. "In attacking the problem again I almost regretted that the struggle was soon to end," Tesla later wrote. "I had so much energy to spare. When I undertook the task it was not with a resolve such as men often make. With me, it was a sacred vow, a ☐uestion of life and death. I knew that I would perish if I failed. Now I felt that the battle was won. Back in the deep recesses of the brain was the solution, but I could not yet give it outward expression."

He would spend the next six years of his life "thinking" about electromagnetic fields and a hypothetical motor powered by alternate-current that would and should work. The thoughts obsessed him, and he was unable to focus on his schoolwork. Professors at the university warned Tesla's father that the young scholar's working and sleeping habits were killing him. But rather than finish his studies, Tesla became a gambling addict, lost all his tuition money, dropped out of school and suffered a nervous breakdown. It would not be his last.

In 1881, Tesla moved to Budapest, after recovering from his breakdown, and he was walking through a park with a friend, reciting poetry, when a vision came to him. There in the park, with a stick, Tesla drew a crude diagram in the dirt—a motor using the principle of rotating magnetic fields created by two or more alternating currents. While AC electrification had been employed before, there would never be a practical, working motor run on alternating current until he invented his induction motor several years later.

In June 1884, Tesla sailed for New York City and arrived with four cents in his pocket and a letter of recommendation from Charles Batchelor—a former employer—to Thomas Edison, which was purported to say, "My Dear Edison: I know two great men and you are one of them. The other is this young man!"

A meeting was arranged, and once Tesla described the engineering work he was doing, Edison, though skeptical, hired him. According to Tesla, Edison offered him $50,000 if he could improve upon the DC generation plants Edison favored. Within a few months, Tesla informed the American inventor that he had indeed improved upon Edison's motors. Edison, Tesla noted, refused to pay up. "When you become a full-fledged American, you will appreciate an American joke," Edison told him.

Tesla promptly quit and took job digging ditches. But it wasn't long before word got out that Tesla's AC motor was worth investing in, and the Western Union Company put Tesla to work in a lab not far from Edison's office, where he designed AC power systems that are still used around the world. "The motors I built there," Tesla said, "were exactly as I imagined them. I made no attempt to improve the design, but merely reproduced the pictures as they appeared to my vision, and the operation was always as I expected."

Tesla patented his AC motors and power systems, which were said to be the most valuable inventions since the telephone. Soon, George Westinghouse, recognizing that Tesla's designs might be just what he needed in his efforts to unseat Edison's DC current, licensed his patents for $60,000 in stocks and cash and royalties based on how much electricity Westinghouse could sell. Ultimately, he won the "War of the Currents," but at a steep cost in litigation and competition for both Westinghouse and Edison's General Electric Company.

Fearing ruin, Westinghouse begged Tesla for relief from the royalties Westinghouse agreed to. "Your decision determines the fate of the Westinghouse Company," he said. Tesla, grateful to the man who had never tried to swindle him, tore up the royalty contract, walking away from millions in royalties that he was already owed and billions that would have accrued in the future. He would have been one of the wealthiest men in the world—a titan of the Gilded Age.

His work with electricity reflected just one facet of his fertile mind. Before the turn of the 20th century, Tesla had invented a powerful coil that was capable of generating high voltages and frequencies, leading to new forms of light, such as neon and fluorescent, as well as X-rays. Tesla also discovered that these coils, soon to be called "Tesla Coils," made it possible to send and receive radio signals. He quickly filed for American patents in 1897, beating the Italian inventor Guglielmo Marconi to the punch.

Tesla continued to work on his ideas for wireless transmissions when he proposed to J.P. Morgan his idea of a wireless globe. After Morgan put up the $150,000 to build the giant transmission tower, Tesla promptly hired the noted architect Stanford White of McKim, Mead, and White in New York. White, too, was smitten with Tesla's idea. After all, Tesla was the highly acclaimed man behind Westinghouse's success with alternating current, and when Tesla talked he was persuasive.

"As soon as completed, it will be possible for a business man in New York to dictate instructions, and have them instantly appear in type at his office in London or elsewhere," Tesla said at the time. "He will be able to call up, from his desk, and talk to any telephone subscriber on the globe, without any change whatever in the existing equipment. An inexpensive instrument, not bigger than a watch, will enable its bearer to hear anywhere, on sea or land, music or song, the speech of a political leader, the address of an eminent man of science or the sermon of an eloquent clergyman, delivered in some other place, however distant. In the same manner any picture, character, drawing or print can be transferred from one to another place. Millions of such instruments can be operated from but one plant of this kind."

White quickly got to work designing Wardenclyffe Tower in 1901, but soon after construction began it became apparent that Tesla was going to run out of money before it was finished. A appeal to Morgan for more money proved fruitless, and in the meantime investors were rushing to throw their money behind Marconi. In December 1901, Marconi successfully sent a signal from England to Newfoundland. Tesla grumbled that the Italian was using 17 of his patents, but litigation eventually favored Marconi and the commercial damage was done. (The U.S. Supreme Court ultimately upheld Tesla's claims, clarifying Tesla's role in the invention of the radio—but not until 1943, after he died.) Thus the Italian inventor was credited as the inventor of the radio and became rich. Wardenclyffe Tower became an 186-foot-tall relic (it would be razed in 1917), and the defeat—Tesla's worst—led to another of his breakdowns. "It is not a dream," Tesla said, "it is a simple feat of scientific electrical engineering, only expensive—blind, faint-hearted, doubting world!"

By 1912, Tesla began to withdraw from that doubting world. He was clearly showing signs of an obsessive-compulsive disorder, and was potentially a high-functioning autistic. He became obsessed with cleanliness and fixated on the number three; he began shaking hands with people and washing his hands—all did in sets of three. He had to have 18 napkins on his table during meals, and would count his steps whenever he walked anywhere. He claimed to have an abnormal sensitivity to sounds, as well as a acute sense of sight, and he later wrote that he had "a violent aversion against the earrings of women," and "the sight of a pearl would almost give me a fit."

Near the end of his life, Tesla became fixated on pigeons, especially a specific white female, which he claimed to love almost as one would love a human being. One night, Tesla claimed the white pigeon visited him through an open window at his hotel, and he believed the bird had come to tell him she was dying. He saw "two powerful beans of light" in the bird's eyes, he later said. "Yes, it was a real light, a powerful, dazzling, blinding light, a light more intense than I had ever produced by the most powerful lamps in my laboratory." The pigeon died in his arms and the inventor claimed that, in that moment, he knew that he had finished his life's work.

Nikola Tesla would go on to make news from time to time while living on the 33rd floor of the New Yorker Hotel. In 1931 he made the cover of Time magazine, which featured his inventions on his 75th birthday. And in 1934, the New York Times reported that Tesla was working on a "Death Beam" capable of knocking 10,000 enemy airplanes out of the sky. He hoped to fund a prototypical defensive weapon in the interest of world peace, but his appeals to J.P. Morgan Jr. and British Prime Minister Neville Chamberlain went nowhere. Tesla did, however, receive a $25,000 check from the Soviet Union, but the project languished. He died in 1943, in debt, although Westinghouse had been paying his room and board at the hotel for years.

CHAPTER 6- THINGS YOU NEVER KNEW ABOUT NIKOLA TESLA

1. HE HAD A TREMENDOUS TALENT FOR VISUALIZING INVENTIONS—BUT WAS ALSO PRONE TO OTHER STRANGE VISIONS.

Tesla was able to visualize objects, including inventions he was building, in his head, down to the minutest detail. His method of working was pretty unorthodox compared to other inventors, as he rarely created sketches or drawings, relying instead on the power of his own imagination to work out details. Beginning in early childhood, Tesla experienced flashes of light, which were sometimes followed by inspiration or solutions to problems. These visions could sometimes take on the character of a spiritual experience, but Tesla, a man of science, discounted any such interpretation, valuing them only for their scientific benefit.

2. HE PIONEERED MANY SIGNIFICANT MODERN INVENTIONS BEYOND ALTERNATING CURRENT.

For many, Tesla is associated with the "War of the Currents"—waged with onetime employer and later rival Thomas Edison—over the form of electricity that would become standard. Edison championed direct current, or DC, while Tesla and ally George Westinghouse fought for alternating current, or AC. AC, of course, eventually won out over DC, despite Edison's attempts to malign Tesla's invention by pushing the electric chair as a method of execution to show how dangerous AC was. However, Tesla also conducted pioneering work in electric light, electric motors, radio, x-ray, remote control, radar, wireless communications, and robotics, and created his famous transformer, the Tesla coil. Tesla was in many cases not properly recognized for his contributions, with other inventors receiving credit for improving on what he began. He obtained around 300 patents in his lifetime.

3. HE HAD EXTREMELY REGULAR, EVEN OBSESSIVE-COMPULSIVE, HABITS, AND WAS A GERMAPHOBE.

Throughout his life, Tesla displayed a formidable work ethic, keeping a regimented schedule. Some claim he slept only two hours a night. He often took his dinner at the same table at Delmonico's in New York, and later at the Waldorf-Astoria hotel. He had a all-consuming fear of germs and required a stack of 18 napkins. He was obsessed with the number three, and was prone to carrying out compulsive rituals related to three. When he was young, he would develop a fit at the sight of pearls, and could not bear to touch hair.

4. HE CLAIMED TO HAVE NEARLY CREATED AN EARTHQUAKE IN MANHATTAN.

Tesla's electro-mechanical oscillator, a steam-powered electrical generator, was developed as a possible replacement for inefficient steam engines used to turn generators but could not compete with steam turbines. Tesla reportedly regaled friends with a tale in which his experiments with the oscillator at his lab at 46 East Houston Street in Manhattan set off vibrations that generated a resonance in several neighboring buildings, shaking the ground and prompting calls to police. When the machine began oscillating at the resonance frequency of his own building, Tesla surmised that he was in danger of creating an earthquake, and allegedly smashed the device with a sledgehammer. The claims—which earned the machine the nickname "Tesla's Earthquake Machine"—were later debunked by Mythbusters (the team felt vibrations from hundreds of feet away using a re-creation of Tesla's machine, but didn't create any earthquakes).

5. HE ELECTRIFIED BUTTERFLIES AND BLEW OUT POWER STATIONS IN COLORADO.

Tesla moved his operations near Colorado Springs in 1899 in order to take advantage of the great amount of space available for experimentation and the free supply of AC power he had been offered thereby the El Paso Power

Company—and because he believed the thin atmosphere might be conducive to his goal of wireless power transmission. Experiments in lab with an 80-foot tower, 142-foot metal mast, and enormous Tesla coil formed massive bolts of artificial lightning that supposedly created thunder and errant sparks 15 miles away, surprising people and frightening horses, and surrounding butterflies with halos of St. Elmo's fire. The bolts also blew out dynamos at a local power company and caused a blackout. It's not clear if Tesla succeeded in the wireless transmission of power, however.

6. HE WAS A SNAPPY DRESSER AND ATTRACTED THE LADIES.

By all accounts, Tesla was a striking individual. At 6 foot 2 and just over 140 pounds, he was very tall and slender, with dark, deep-set eyes. He was also a fashionable and fastidious dresser, and while he could be reclusive while deeply engaged in work, he was fascinating company when he felt like being social. Not only did he attract the friendship of famous people like Mark Twain, but he also drew the attentions of women, some of whom confessed to being "madly in love" with him. Much of Tesla's personal life remains a mystery, however, and he never married.

7. HE DIDN'T REALLY SIT IN A ROOM SURROUNDED BY LIGHTNING BOLTS.

That famous photo of Tesla sitting on a chair in his laboratory and calmly examining his notes while tremendous bolts of lightning flash around him was likely the result of a double exposure. Yet the image, taken at his Colorado lab and used as publicity to generate capital for new projects, captures the public's fascination with a scientist whose prowess made him seem a magician to many.

8. HE WANTED TO ILLUMINATE THE ENTIRE EARTH, LITERALLY.

Tesla believed that his work had the potential to light the earth's atmosphere, banishing darkness and bringing in a new era of light. He theorized that gases in Earth's upper atmosphere were capable of carrying high-freuency electrical currents, and successful transmission of such currents there could create a "terrestrial night light" that would make shipping lanes and airports safer and illuminate whole cities. But like most of Tesla's loftier aims, this goal was never realized, and its possibility remains unproven.

9. THE SECRET PURPOSE OF HIS GIANT TOWER ON LONG ISLAND WAS THE WIRELESS TRANSMISSION OF POWER.

As the 20th century arrived, Tesla was locked in a race with Italian inventor Guglielmo Marconi to be the first to transmit messages across the Atlantic Ocean. Tesla began securing funding, much of it coming from financier J.P. Morgan, to build a wireless transmission station on Long Island with a massive, 186-foot tower. The station would be called Wardenclyffe. Tesla, however, had his own agenda. He wanted to use Wardenclyffe to fulfill his long-held dream of transmitting electricity wirelessly. When Marconi beat Tesla to the punch in 1901, transmitting the letters across the Atlantic with much more modest equipment, Tesla was forced to reveal his ulterior motives to Morgan and to beg for additional funding to complete his tower. Morgan, however, indicated that he was no longer interested in the project and pulled his support. This move, along with other factors, would ultimately spell the project's doom.

10. WARDENCLYFFE IS BEING TURNED INTO A MUSEUM.

Wardenclyffe fell into disrepair after the collapse of Tesla's ambitions there and destruction of its tower in 1917. The main building, designed by architect Stanford White, remained and was alternately left abandoned or used for industrial purposes. Nonprofit group The Tesla Science Center at Wardenclyffe began a successful crowdfunding campaign in 2012 with the goal of buying the property, and closed the deal in 2013. A plan is underway to convert the site into a Tesla museum and science education center, with work ongoing. The site is not yet open to the public, but visitors are allowed for special events, like Tesla's birthday celebration in July.

11. HE SPOKE 8 LANGUAGES

No doubt hastened by his eidetic—commonly known as photographic—memory, Tesla was fluent in 8 different languages: Serbo-Croatian, English, Czech, German, French, Hungarian, Italian and Latin. Linguists refer to such a person as a "hyper polyglot", or someone who can speak more than six languages with great proficiency.

12. HE HAD A DEATH RAY

To put it a bit more accurately, Tesla possessed an intricate design plan for a death ray – a particle beam/directed-energy weapon he named "Teleforce" — that was meant to be used during World War One to wipe out whole armies.

He described the invention thusly: "[The nozzle would] send concentrated beams of particles through the free air, of such tremendous energy that they will bring down a fleet of 10,000 enemy airplanes at a distance of 200 miles from a defending nation's border and will cause armies to drop dead in their tracks." Tesla worked to bring Teleforce to fruition until the day he died.

13. HE HAD A STRANGE RELATIONSHIP WITH PIGEONS

While Tesla appears to have been unable to foster feelings for humans and has thus been described as asocial, perhaps his aversion to people had less to do with his lack of emotion and more to do with the fact that they lacked feathers.

Like many people do, Tesla would feed the populous gray colored birds at the park. Even after he was too ill to do it himself, he hired others to do it for him. He would often bring sick or injured pigeons back to the hotel where he lived in his later years, and nurse them back to health.

He grew especially fond of one little bird, and said this about her; "I loved that pigeon as man loves a woman, and she loved me. As long as I had her, there was a purpose to my life."

14. HE DIED BROKE AND ALONE

A sad, empty ending for man filled to the brim with brilliance, Tesla died on January 7th, 1943 from coronary thrombosis in the New Yorker hotel room that had served as his home for a decade. The hotel maid discovered his body two days later, after she chose to ignore a "do not disturb" sign placed on his door.

Though he sold his AC electrical patents, Tesla died in debt because he self-funded many of his own projects that never ended up seeing the light of day. He died at the age of 87.

15. MANY OF HIS INVENTIONS REMAIN CLASSIFIED

Upon his death, most of Tesla's belongings were taken by the Office of Alien Property – even though he was legal citizen of the United States. And by "most", we mean what has been described as a "railroad boxcar" full of Tesla's materials. After a time, some items were released to his family, while others ended up in the Tesla museum, located in Belgrade, Serbia (where his ashes are also kept).

Some of Tesla's documents and papers still remain classified, and while people have re uested items via the Freedom of Information Act, those items are heavily redacted before their release. As a result, people tend to wonder what else Nikola Tesla had up his sleeve—like a device that would lead to free energy— before his death.

16-HE WAS BORN DURING A LIGHTNING STORM

Nikola Tesla was born approximately at midnight, between July 9 and July 10, 856, during a lightning storm. During Tesla birth, and according to the story old by his family, the midwife wrung her hands and declared the lightning a bad omen. "This child will be a child of darkness", she reportedly said, to which Tesla's mother replied: "No. He will be a child of light."

17-HE AND EDISON WERE RIVALS, BUT NOT SWORN ENEMIES

Many have pictured Tesla and inventor Thomas Edison as enemies but their relationship has been misrepresented. Early in his career, Tesla worked for Edison, designing direct current generators, but famously ⬚uit to pursue his own project: the alternating current induction motor. Sure, they were on different sides of the so-called "Current Wars," with Edison pushing for direct current and Tesla for alternating current. But considers them the Steve Jobs and Bill Gates of their time: one the brilliant marketer and businessman, and the other a visionary and "tech guy."

18-HE HAD THE IDEA FOR SMARTPHONE TECHNOLOGY IN 1901

Tesla may have had a brilliant mind, but he was not as good at reducing his ideas to practice. In the race to develop transatlantic radio, Tesla described to his funder and business partner, J.P. Morgan, new means of instant communication that involved gathering stock ⬚uotes and telegram messages, funneling them to his laboratory, where he would encode them and assign them each a new fre⬚uency. That fre⬚uency would be broadcast to a device that would fit in your hand, he explained. In other words, Tesla had envisioned the smart phone and wireless internet, Carlson said, adding that of all of his ideas, that was the one that stopped him in his tracks.

19-HE HAD PHOTOGRAPHIC MEMORY

Tesla had what's known as a photographic memory. He was known to memorize books and images and stockpile visions for inventions in his head. He also had a powerful imagination and the ability to visualize in three dimensions, which he reportedly used to control the terrifying vivid nightmares from which he suffered from as a child. It's in part what makes him such a mystical and eccentric character in popular culture, Carlson said. He was also known for having excessive hygiene habits, born out of a near-fatal bout of cholera as a teenager.

20- PEARLS DROVE HIM CRAZY

Tesla could not stand the sight of pearls, to the extent that he refused to speak to women wearing them. When his secretary wore pearl jewelry, he sent her home for the day. No one knows why he had such an aversion, but Tesla had a very particular sense of style and aesthetics, Carlson said, and believed that, in order to be successful, one needed to look successful. He wore white gloves to dinner every night and prided himself on being a "dapper dresser."

CHAPTER 7- SUMMARY

Born in the Austrian Empire (now Croatia) in 1856, Nikola Tesla was one of the foremost inventors of the twentieth century with an amazingly long list of devices coming out of his fertile mind, including a viable free energy apparatus. Tesla traveled to the United States and in 1891 and became an American citizen. He died penniless in 1943 in New York City.

Tesla was most famous for his work with electricity, most often in the areas of electromagnetism and electromechanical engineering. Tesla was hired by Thomas Edison shortly after Tesla came to America in 1888 but after a time, his relationship soured with Edison and Tesla decided to form his own company called Tesla Electric Light and Manufacturing.

A celebrity then but almost unknown these days, Tesla's inventions and knowledge are at the root of much of present day and perhaps even future advances. This is even more astonishing when you consider that all of this happened roughly 100 years ago! Tesla was a committed promoter of alternating current as opposed to direct current as was championed by Edison for the transmission of electrical current. The catch with direct (DC) current is that it can't be sent more than few city blocks before losing voltage. AC current can be sent for very long distances at very high voltages and then stepped down by voltage transformers at or near its final destination.

All of Edison's devices were centered on DC current and he was unwilling to dismiss of the notion of having DC current grow to be the standard for the transmission of electricity. Edison defended his position on DC current by stating that electrical motors could not operate on alternating (AC) current. Tesla answered that drawback by inventing the induction electric motor, still utilized today, that operates on AC power. Edison's commitment to DC power was slow to diminish and so a kind of war started between Edison and Tesla after Tesla went into alliance with George Westinghouse for the purpose of developing AC as the standard for electrical power transmission. Tesla and Westinghouse eventually were victorious in the "current war" and alternating current became the standard and remains so today.

Tesla's devices included wireless communications, although Gugliemo Marconi, an Italian inventor, beat Tesla to the punch by sending the first transatlantic radio signal. Tesla also did pioneering work with X-rays, lasers, cellular technology, neon and high voltage devices. Tesla also made early contributions in the sciences of ballistics, theoretical physics, nuclear physics, radar, robotics, remote control and computer science. Many of Tesla's inventions were powered by another creation of his that was known as the "Tesla coil."

He also developed a way of sending electricity through the air, utilizing the conductivity of the earth to run vehicles distantly. One of his dreams was to have automobiles powered remotely by a free energy transmitting station. The electricity would be transmitted through the air with the earth making up the other half of the circuit. This was never developed on a practical level.

Other Tesla endeavors included the creation of the initial hydroelectric power plant (in association with George Westinghouse) located at Niagara Falls and the AC electric lighting of the 1893 World's Fair. Helped by investment from J.P Morgan, Tesla built an experimental electricity transmission tower called the Wardenclyffe Tower in 1901. When J.P. Morgan discovered that one of the uses of Tesla's tower would be the generation of free electricity, he pulled back his financing because he realized that the very lucrative business of commercial power generation would become obsolete and he refused to let that take place.

The loss of funding for Wardenclyffe Tower came as terrible news to Tesla. After Tesla's death, all of his paperwork and designs were locked up by an agency of the Federal Government on the orders of J. Edgar Hoover, then head of the F.B.I. Most of Tesla's inventions were far ahead of his time and represented a real financial threat to those who stood to profit from the existing technology of the day. Because of this, Tesla was deliberately "erased" from history and his name is only now becoming known again.

n the present, as the humanity search for low-cost sources of non-polluting electrical power, Tesla's re-emergence into public awareness may be timed perfectly. Tesla truly did learn the secrets of free energy and his plans for an uncomplicated, cheap free energy device are now available to the public once more.

No doubt, great progress has been and is being made in the areas of solar and wind electric power generation but, for the most part, electricity still comes from fossil fuels. Home solar systems are still unaffordable for most homeowners as are home windmills. Tesla's free energy apparatus, is constructed from widely available electrical parts, has no moving parts and claims to use cosmic rays as a source of power.

It's amazing that one individual come up with so many ingenious and practical concepts and inventions in a single life span. That, strangely, may have something to do with a mental condition that Tesla suffered from for most of his life. Tesla stated that he was prone to seeing blinding flashes of light and that he saw visions of new ideas and answers to problems at the same time. He said that these flashes were almost universally triggered by a single word he read or heard that remained in his consciousness.

Towards the end of his life, Tesla also struggled with obsessive-compulsive disorder that featured a obsessive fear of germs and the need to have the important numbers in his life (such as his hotel room number 3327) be divisible by 3. In spite of his mental afflictions, Tesla appeared to make positive use of them as did another obsessive-compulsive giant of the twentieth century, Howard Hughes.

THE END

Printed in Great Britain
by Amazon